GW00645518

LETTERS TO A LADY

Edition 2003
Copyright © 2001, Philip Leonard Baker.

Biblical references are in the New International Version unless otherwise indicated.

Artwork & Design by Belinda McCullough
BAM Graphic Design . Western Australia . T . [618] 9343 5874

Printed in Australia by Hyde Park Press, Richmond, South Australia

All enquiries regarding this publication and Phil Baker's speaking engagements to be made to:
Inside Out Resources Inc.
PO Box 1339, South Perth, Western Australia, 6951
Email: inoutinc@bigpond.net.au
Refer to back pages for more information concerning the author, Philip Baker.

National Library of Australia . Canberra . Australia
ISBN: 0 9577020 3 5

"In his Letters To A Lady, Philip Baker has presented Proverbs 31 in an incredibly creative, inspiring and beautiful way. He seems to understand the value and honour that God gave the woman and is encouraging the reader to see that as well. Not bad for a guy! With his humour and practical insight your eyes will also be opened to the incredible treasure that woman is."

Holly Wagner

Author of Dumb Things He Does/Dumb Things She Does & God Chicks...

"Letters to a Lady' is a beautiful yet unique collection of 22 verses from one of my favourite chapters in the Bible. I believe the Proverbs 31 woman is the blueprint for a magnificent life in God, so I love the way Phil has added to the revelation of the ever-unfolding picture. It is a delight to read such powerful insights in an exquisitely presented book."

Bobbie Houston

Hillsong Church, Sydney, Australia

"I am absolutely fascinated by this new book of yours, resplendent in its superb production. Never have I had such insight into the Hebrew alphabet, and never so much into Proverbs 31. You have pulled off an absolute tour de force! Well done."

Michael Green

Author of over 10 books including Evangelism Through The Local Church and You Must Be Joking

"Letters to A Lady is an exquisite writing by Phillip Baker on the Proverbs 31 woman. It is not only a beautiful gift to give to someone, it is also an excellent teaching tool for Women's groups as well as smaller group settings. It is full of insight and practical wisdom that can be applied to every day life and I highly recommend it to all age groups."

Maree De Jong
Christian Life Centre Auckland, New Zealand

"I love this book! As a woman, mother of three daughters and leader of women, I have found this book to be an invaluable treasure. I have thoroughly enjoyed discovering the amazing attributes of the Proverbs 31 woman with a fresh new perspective as Philip Baker has so cleverly presented it."

Helen Burns
Victory Christian Centre, Vancouver, Canada

"WOW! Only you could pull off a book like this!!!! It is absolutely amazing FANTASTICO. I was very impressed with the book, it is typically Phil-funny, sensitive, challenging and EXTREMELY well presented in a post-modern, out-of-the-box sort of way."

Nicole Conner
Waverley Christian Fellowship, Melbourne, Australia

"What a great book! I read it in one night…apart from providing me with some excellent sermon preparation avoidance material, I loved it from start to finish! Firstly let me say that I love the presentation! Then when I got inside I found that it actually said something intelligent as well! (Always a bonus with Christian books).

I had never heard about Proverbs 31 being an acrostic and so it was all new revelation to me, presented with intelligent humour and great insight.
It will be among those books that I treasure and read again and again, just because the reading of it is such a pleasurable experience. It's on the shelf next to 'Now We Are Six' by A.A. Milne, which is truly an honoured place. Well done for pushing the boundaries by combining art, humour, taste AND good teaching in one book!"

Jane Evans
Paradise Community Church, Adelaide, Australia

"Thanks so much for your new book – I LOVE IT! It's beautiful (very important from a woman's perspective) and completely interesting. You are an author in the truest sense…it's a 'work of art' and an obvious labour of love."

Di Wilson
Author of Fat Free Forever, Fat Free Forever Tips, Fat Free Forever Cookbook and Easy Exercise For Everyone

foreword by
Darlene Zschech

"When this beautiful book 'Letters to a Lady' was placed in my hands, I immediately fell in love with the message, and the value and dignity it placed on the role of 'woman' on the earth.

Phil's style of communication is current, stimulating, so very clever, gloriously honouring, and will bless any woman, of any age, in any stage of life.

Phil and his divine wife Heather, like Mark and I, are the proud parents of three amazing daughters, and we cherish Godly teaching, that would give them tools to allow them to shine throughout their entire lifetime.

This awesome Proverbs 31 woman, although she seems too wonderful for words, is given as a beautiful blueprint from heaven, as our mentor, friend, mother, sister and helpmate.

The art of womanhood is not only very possible, but very accessible.

Be blessed my friends, Read on..."

Darlene Zschech
Hillsong Church, Sydney, Australia

letters

to a lady

letters

to a lady

philip baker

acknowledgements

First of all I would like to acknowledge one of my Bible School teachers, Bob Yandian, whose message on the Virtuous Woman, which I heard in 1979, gave me the initial idea for this book.

To Mark Cullen and Penny Webb, who reignited this idea when I preached a message along these lines on Mother's Day 2000.

I must also mention, of course, the key women in my life; my wonderful wife, Heather and my three daughters, Jazmin, Temily and Isabel.

Not many men write books about the power of the woman but then again, not many men are surrounded by so many powerful women… I actually wanted to write a book about powerful men, but I didn't know any!

"She seemed to know, to accept, to welcome her position, the citadel of the family, the strong place that could not be taken. And since old Tom and the children could not know hurt or fear unless she acknowledged hurt or fear, she had practised denying them in herself. And since, when a joyful thing happened, they looked to see whether joy was on her, it was her habit to build up laughter out of inadequate materials. But better than joy was calm. Imperturbability could be depended upon. And from her great and humble position in the family, she had taken dignity and a clean, calm beauty. From her position as healer, her hands had grown sure and cool and quiet; from her position as arbiter she had become as remote and faultless in judgement as a goddess. She seemed to know that if she swayed, the family shook, and if she ever really deeply wavered or despaired the family would fall, the family will to function would be gone."

The Grapes of Wrath
John Steinbeck

PENGUIN BOOKS, LONDON 2000 P. 77.

Table of Letters

introduction

Let me confess from the outset that I have two main passions in my life… letters and women.

The former are the tools of my trade, being a pastor, speaker and author.

The latter… well I'm surrounded by the latter. I have three daughters, one wife, two mothers, one mother-in-law, four sisters, at least 25 staff members, three board members, one dog and one cat, all of which are female… I have only one thing to say… HELP!

It may come then as no surprise that I feel uniquely qualified to write a book that not only briefly describes the hidden meanings of the Hebrew alphabet but does so within the context of describing the virtuous woman.

Proverbs Chapter 31 verses 10 to 31 is one of a handful of biblical acrostics[i]. Simply said, an acrostic is a Hebrew ABC. Each of these 22 verses, describing the noble woman, begins with a different Hebrew letter from aleph (verse 10 - the equivalent to our 'A'), through to tau (the equivalent to our 'Z'). Hebrew – unlike English – has 22 letters, so it all works out pretty well. What is even more interesting is that each Hebrew letter is a picture[ii], and that picture more often than not has a meaning. What makes this really exciting is that the meaning of the letter corresponds to the teaching of each verse. The original reason for acrostics was to aid in memorisation. In the same way that it would be easier to memorise 26 alphabetically arranged vegetables than it would 26 arbitrary ones. So… it was hoped men the world over would be able to memorise 22 great things about women. Alas… the male of the species gave up after three letters, and the wisdom of Proverbs 31 was lost to men and women alike. So history continued without the input of this wisdom. Thus, we experienced the cultural disempowerment of women, the increasing of an entrenched male chauvinism and James Bond. Anyway… that was until this book awoke a new generation around the world to the truth of the virtuous woman!

the

letters

letter one

aleph

Proverbs 31:10

"Who can find a virtuous woman? For her price is far above rubies."

[KJV]

"A good woman is hard to find, and worth far more than diamonds."

[THE MESSAGE]

aleph

We begin with a summary, a simple statement that encapsulates all that is to follow. Indeed verses 11 – 31 are merely the commentary, an explanation, a detailed analysis, a picture [if you like] of the character and characteristics of this virtuous woman.

It is also interesting to note that this passage extolling the wonders of the woman, are the closing thoughts in what is probably considered to be one of the greatest books on wisdom ever to have been written. In fact throughout the book, wisdom is personified as a lady and the fool, simpleton and the lazy are unfortunately all too often characterised in the male gender. Now obviously, I feel it would be wrong to read too much into this!

If feminism is defined as treating ladies as equals in every area of life then certainly the Book of Proverbs would come down firmly on the pro-feminist position. It is all the rage, of course, at the moment to try to move the traditional idea and concept of God away from being male and church culture from being male gender dominated. Certainly scripture describes God as having both male and female characteristics. Of course, if God is God, then he transcends all narrow gender definitions. However, secretly, I feel such debate is a ploy of the devil. She will try to bring division into the church whenever and wherever she can!

However, away from such musings. The content of this volume is, you'll be most relieved to know, not about such matters. It is, however, clearly about not just how God sees women but how the male of the species should treasure and esteem her as well. A myth that has been perpetrated by a sort of religious chauvinism, which is still alive and well in many churches around the world, is that the woman's place is not only in the home but is intrinsically subservient to the male as well. Jesus, the early church, and the writer of the Book of Proverbs would decry such a philosophy at the top of their collective voices.

This virtuous woman, as we shall see, is both a homemaker and a businesswoman. Both aggressive and tender. She is both sexually alive and spiritually alert. She is what God designed a woman to be. Her description is not given in such a way as to hold up an ideal and thereby condemn or depress all those who are falling short of it. It is rather given to inspire, to paint a picture of what could be and declare that every woman has great nobility and sadly an often unappreciated value.

To declare to every man that the most wonderful, the most valuable, the most beautiful, the most fascinating and fulfilling endeavour he could ever experience will be discovered within a relationship with the crown and glory of God's creation. The lady who walks softly by his side.

This introductory verse then,

"A virtuous woman who can find, her price is far above rubies."

is given almost as an invitation to the male of the species. She is there, yet she hides in the garden waiting to be found. An understanding of her nobility and a pledge to esteem and treat her in accordance with her value will enable us to truly find her.

The Hebrew letter that begins this verse is, of course, the first in the Hebrew alphabet the letter, 'aleph'. The 'aleph' was a picture of oxen ploughing. Ah, of course, I see it now! I hear you exclaiming… I guess the original 'aleph' actually looked like oxen ploughing. Now we just have to believe the lexical historians. The ox throughout scripture had several different meanings. First and foremost it literally meant strength. The ox was the chief working animal on the farm because of its strength and is renowned for its ability to sustain an incredibly heavy workload.

The ox was also a sign of prosperity. This was because oxen didn't come cheap. Indeed, in the sacrificial system, referred to in Leviticus, the rich were asked to sacrifice an ox. Then, in accordance with economic worth, people were allowed to sacrifice a cow, a goat, a sheep, all the way down to a dove. Leviticus Chapter 5 makes the point that if you can't afford a dove then so much meal is considered satisfactory. In another passage in I Kings 19:19 we discover Elisha ploughing with 12 head of oxen. His family farm was obviously a very successful one, which makes his subsequent calling into ministry by Elijah even more noteworthy. In that, what he was leaving was in all probability a sizeable inheritance.

Notice how the text of the verse

"A virtuous woman who can find, her price is far above rubies."

is mirrored by the Hebrew letter and its meaning. And as we have already discussed, the rest of this acrostic simply delineates how much value, how much strength, how much prosperity and worth this virtuous woman actually brings through her life to touch the lives of those around.

The comparison is made in the King James version of the Bible, to rubies. Other translations speak of jewels [Good News Bible], gems

[Living Bible], pearls [Jerusalem Bible], and even coral [New English Bible]. I'm not sure whether I like that last one – it could mean of course that she is very colourful or she is sharp, cutting and dangerous!

The point of all these is that they are not found on the surface, they are underground or underwater and as we have already hinted at, only those who are prepared to search, to expend energy and effort, will see her true beauty. I am writing, of course, from a male point of view, yet this is equally true from the female perspective, in that, within us all are deep and wonderful things. Our responsibility is to unearth them. To not allow the nay-sayers to declare that nothing is there and simply throw more dirt onto our lives. Unfortunately today, most of us find it easy to believe what others say and difficult to believe our own aspirations and dreams.

Just this last week as I was standing at the checkout of our local supermarket, a gentleman walked up to me who recognised me and asked if I had written any more books. After he had gone, the young checkout operator, she must have been 19 or 20, said with a look of great interest, "Oh, you're a writer." She then went on to say she had always wanted to be a writer and in fact had started a book but then someone who was close to her had told her it was a stupid idea. I told her most of the great books of the world were written by people who simply hadn't listened to what everybody had said, and encouraged her to pick up pen once more. Yet here is one illustration of what must happen every day to multiple lives… the treasure within is pushed deeper down and as a result the gift, the virtue, the real person never gets to the surface.

One attorney tried to assess the value of a wife and mother. He noted that she was chauffeur, gardener, family counsellor, maintenance person, cleaner, housekeeper, cook, errand runner, bookkeeper, manager, interior decorator, dietician, P.R., hostess as well as working in an external job.

The yearly salary for this unpaid work, he figured at a bare minimum, being around US$100,000 per annum. If the majority of women were paid for what they actually do, there would hardly be a house in the country that could afford her. Let me be quick to add, just in case my wife is reading this, that I am not suggesting that people should be paid, either men or women, for what they do in these capacities. I am simply making the point that we should never underestimate the value of her role.

letter two

beth

Proverbs 31:11

"The heart of her husband doth safely trust in her, so that he shall have no need of spoil"

[KJV]

"Her husband can trust her, and she will greatly enrich his life."

[NLT]

beth

This Hebrew letter is a picture of a house. In fact, the Hebrew word for house is Bait. The letter was simply a picture of the sound.

The term 'house' in scripture rarely refers simply to the physical building. Rather it is all about what a house is. Probably the best English word to describe this would be the word, 'home'. We think of the House of God, the House of Israel, how the Philippian jailer and 'his house' were baptised by Paul and Silas. House was all about family, relationships, community and security.

She has the ability to turn the house into a home. She is a star around which everyone else orbits. A cartoon that best summarises this concept is one of a 6-year-old boy on the phone speaking to an unknown caller saying, 'Mum is in the hospital, so the twins, and Roxy, and Billy, and Sally and the dog and me and Dad are all home alone.'"

I am reminded of the film, <u>Primary Colours</u>, in which several of the characters one night at a barbecue restaurant in a southern American state begin to reminisce about their mothers. Passions rose, time stood still and the character playing the President's wife turned to the young intern [No, not that intern!] and said, "Don't worry, this is a traditional southern Mummathon. They have been known to go all night."

This woman engenders trust, she brings security to a world that so often lacks it. The virtuous woman is not playing games, she is not on the prowl looking for the affair, happy to move from one relationship to the next. There is a depth here that encourages trust and commitment. Without it the relationship is on a timer.

For a house to be secure it must have firm foundations. She was not so desperate to find a mate or build a family, that she fast tracked the construction in a similar way to the foolish man Jesus spoke about who built his house on sand. I think in our relational world, who we are is the foundation on which we should build. Regardless of gender, if we think we will discover ourselves or become healthy as a person by getting married, then we have simply brought an unhealthy foundation into marriage.

Good marriages, healthy marriages are all about two healthy people getting together. We are all, of course, on a journey of recovery yet there is a time when the primary job is getting right on the inside first before the secondary job of finding a life-long partner and building a house together.

So the virtuous woman has done this. She is who she is. She has dealt with baggage, discovered herself and connected with God. For these reasons her husband is right to safely trust in her.

letter three

gimel

Proverbs 31:12

"She will do him good and not evil
all the days of her life."

[KJV]

"She comforts, encourages, and does him only
good as long as there is life within her."

[AMP]

gimel

The 'gimel' was a picture of a camel. Today, to most of us, the camel is an unfamiliar animal usually only seen in a zoo or a desert. Yet its importance in the ancient world cannot be underestimated. They were not fast animals but they were reliable. When everyone else was dying of thirst or stumbling through exhaustion, the camel kept plodding on. Consistency, and as a result dependability, are the key thoughts here. She will do him good and not evil ALL the days of her life.

At the time of writing this book, I have been married 17 years. I would hate to think over the next 30 or so years of my marriage, either myself or my wife Heather would stop putting energy into the our relationship. Doing good takes effort. Most couples put in a lot of effort in the early stages. The trick is to keep on making such deposits over the long term.

We have a little joke between the two of us as to who will outlive whom. I am convinced I will be at her funeral and she's convinced she will be at mine. [Just a side thought – it is important to go to other people's funerals or else they won't come to yours!] "Anyway, honey,

I have finally found a biblical verse to back my position." Notice here, it says, she will do him good all the days of her life. Implication – he lives longer than she does… however, if this camel analogy really applies, she will simply keep plodding on leaving me far behind.

You see the whole concept that the woman is a weaker vessel is a myth. The point is they are not. It's just that we guys have to treat them as if they were.*iii* The truth is, they live longer, deal with anxiety better and have babies. In comparison to that, Rambo is a sissy. We men are a little like the guy in <u>Lawrence of Arabia</u> who fell off his camel; on his own he was history.

The virtuous woman then is strong. She keeps on going, like a Duracell – she lasts longer. Like Susie Maroney, the famed Australian swimmer who recently swam from Cuba to Florida, she has the ability to keep on going when many of the males of the species would have vanished quietly beneath the surface.

It reminds me a little of one of the episodes in the well-known <u>7-Up</u> series made for television by BBC. These documentaries visited a group of children when they were seven, and then every seven years after that, to see how their lives, beliefs and circumstances had changed. Initially it was simply an attempt to see whether or not the old saying,

"Give me a child until he is seven and I will give you the man", was true. The series however grew in popularity until the original purpose was almost forgotten, as we were all simply curious about these other people's lives.

In the episode 42-Up, this dependability aspect came clearly to the fore. Most of the ladies in the series were raising their kids, finding jobs, making life happen. Whereas many of the men who had been in their lives had taken off on a forlorn quest for freedom. The women were still there, rock solid, seldom complaining, doing what needed to be done, meeting the pain in life with persistence and purpose. Taking all of the responsibility on their wide and strengthening shoulders.

letter four

daleth

Proverbs 31:13

"*She seeketh wool and flax, and worketh willingly with her hands.*"

[KJV]

"*She looks for wool and flax, and works with her hands in delight.*"

[NASB]

daleth

The 'daleth' was a picture of an open door when viewed from above. It is actually one of the few Hebrew words where you can actually really see it, unless you count the 'gimel'. Which everyone recognises looks exactly like a camel!

The New International Version translates this, "She selects wool and flax and works with eager hands." The virtuous woman has made the decision in her life that she won't just do, but she will be willing to do. The open door stands for decisions and the greatest decisions we can make in our life have to do with our attitude.

Willingness is a frame of mind. It is a decision to whistle while we work, to see life in terms not of what it brings to us but in terms of what we bring to it. To realise that the substance of our world has not so much to do with circumstances as it has to do with our interpretation of the circumstances. One can be miserable in a mansion and happy in a hut. Indeed, the suicide rate amongst the rich and famous is far higher per head of population than amongst the poor and anonymous. This lady understands she has the power of decision and with it she fashions her life. Life is not so much about chance as it is about choice. We were not designed to be creatures of our circumstances – they are designed to be subservient to our decisions.

I used to be indecisive… but now I'm not so sure!

I think it is true, however, that many of us fail to appreciate this incredible power that we all have within our grasp. There are many different kinds of powers in the world today. There is the power of money; charisma; position; and sexuality; there is terrorist power, conventional armed power, and nuclear power; there is the power of our past and the power of our dreams. The Bible speaks of the power of God, the power of temptation, the power of the evil one. We trust that our lives are touched by the power of love, our savings by the power of compound interest and that our children are well balanced through the power of values… and if that doesn't work, the leveraged power of an early curfew.

Yet all these powers are subservient to the God-given power we all have within us – the power of decision. However, even though this power is so potent, most treat it casually or employ it without the safety catch on. This lady of Proverbs Chapter 31 does not shirk from the power of decision, she uses it intentionally. If she is going to work for her family she is going to work with a will, not just endure each passing hour, but dance lightly within it.

With this attitude to life we quickly discover that the fun, the fulfilment and the fruit are the result of not so much what we do but how we do it. In the book of Isaiah 1:19 God in speaking to Israel declared that, "if they are willing and obedient they will eat the good of the land". Just being obedient is not good enough. In the New Testament children are exhorted to honour and obey their parents. The twelve-year-old who cleans her room obediently yet with a bad attitude will never receive the praise of her parents or other more tangible rewards that parents love to give kids when they smilingly obey. [Please note, Jazmin, Temily and Isabel, this sentence was for you!]

This particular characteristic imbues the life with strength. All of us at various times can become overwhelmed by the responsibility of life, the task ahead and the nurturing of relationships. Add to this the vital importance and complexity of parenting well, organising efficiently and resourcing the physical, emotional and spiritual needs of the lives around us. Is it any wonder that many choose simply to exist, to do enough to get by and not advance their life in the direction of their dreams.

It was the Italian writer, Gramsci, who best encapsulated how this concept of willingness could come to the rescue when everything within us wanted to quit, when he wrote, "We have a pessimism of the intellect but an optimism of the will."

The 'daleth' then is the open door of decision, a door which remains open, for right decisions require refreshing day by day. It may also be worthwhile to point out that the wool and the flax that our lady is looking for in this particular verse are so she can make clothes for the family. Today the task of getting clothes is called shopping and, from what I understand, is a far more pleasurable activity.

letter five

h e

Proverbs 31:14

"She is like the merchants' ships; she bringeth her food from afar."
[KJV]

"She's like a trading ship that sails to faraway places and brings back exotic surprises."
[THE MESSAGE]

he

The 'he' was a picture of a window. It is, if you like, very similar to the 'beth' picture of the house except this time on its end and with a small opening.

A window enables us to see. It has to do with our vision – what we are looking for, our perspective on life. Vision is the ability to see beyond the obvious and is based, not so much on what actually is, but on what we are searching for. William Blake put it this way, "We see not with, but through the eye."[iv]   In a previous book, Attitudes of Amazing Achievers,[v] I devoted a whole chapter to the subject of vision and how the eye is the window to the soul. That what we are looking for in life is all about who we are on the inside.

The critical person will always be critical because the problem is not on the outside but on the inside. Once we fix up what he or she was critical about, they will simply find something new to criticise because they are actually looking for the flaw, for the failure, for the foible. The positive person, on the other hand, is looking for things to praise, to be encouraged by or to gain hope from. Negativity and optimism then are all about us and have little to do with objective reality. The rub is that optimism and pessimism both have the ability to change reality to conform to what was seen in the first place.

The letter 'he' then is about vision and perspective.

"She is like the merchants' ships; she bringeth her food from afar."

Food was obviously available closer at hand, at the local market. So it seems that either accessibility or speed were not the primary considerations. It is well documented in ancient times that the merchants would bring the best the world had to offer into Solomon's kingdom. I Kings 10:22 states, "The king had a fleet of trading ships at sea along with the ships of Hiram. Once every three years it returned carrying gold, silver, ivory, apes and baboons." Now I am not too sure what the big deal was with the apes and baboons. I am simply making the point that he brought the finest from wherever it was. If someone wanted a baboon it was going to be the best baboon money could buy.

In the same way, the virtuous woman is looking for the best. She is not quick to compromise. Her perspective is one of, "if it is worth doing, it is worth doing well" - a perspective of excellence. The point being made here is not an economic one, for excellence is simply doing the best with what you have, regardless of whether it is cooking a meal, loving our spouse or working at a job. We owe it to one another, especially in the context of marriage, to give of ourselves fully. Half-heartedness will not only defraud those around oneself but will slowly shrink the boundaries of one's life as well. If you give your best now, your best will simply get better tomorrow. If you hold back, even that which you have will be diminished.

The virtuous woman understands this, so her vision is to give one hundred percent of herself to those she loves. Now the corollary of this is that she deserves such treatment in return. The 'going the extra mile' culture is one in which she is not merely the giver but also the recipient. She does deserve that night out, those flowers, that drive across town for the take-away rice pudding to fulfil a craving at ten-thirty in the evening.

The point, which the virtuous woman so ably makes, is that it's not about distance and it's not about time........ it's about the person.

letter six

v a v

Proverbs 31:15

"*She riseth also while it is yet night
and giveth meat to her household, and
a portion to her maidens.*"

[KJV]

"*She's up before dawn, preparing breakfast
for her family and organising her day.*"

[THE MESSAGE]

vav

The 'vav' is a picture of a hook or a nail. It would be true to say, in respect to the virtuous woman, that the whole household hangs on her.

I used to point this verse out to my wife, in particular that section where it talks about the fact that she is up before the sun. Heather was quick to read the second part of the verse and insisted that if I employed maid servants, then maybe she would get up a little bit earlier, because when she had given the maid servants all the jobs that she had lined up, she could go back to bed!

She controls the atmosphere in the home. The hopes, the esteem of her children and husband often are inspired and nurtured by her. I love something that Picasso said, "When I was a child my Mum said to me, 'If you become a soldier, you'll be a general. If you become a monk you'll end up as the Pope.' Instead I became a painter and I wound up as Picasso." Or in a similar vein, Thomas Edison, when a young boy, brought home a teacher's note which said, "You're child is dumb, we can't do anything for him." The mother wrote back, "You do not understand my boy... I will teach him myself." What a difference a lady makes.

Now I am aware, in the process of writing this that the mistake and assumption could be made that this poor woman is surrounded by a bunch of no-hopers. "Where is her husband?" I hear you muttering. She is looking after him, he's sleeping in, she's out buying stuff from around the world, turning the house into a home, bringing value into his world and doing it all with a smile on her face while he is just twiddling his thumbs and thanking God that he has found this virtuous woman.

Unfortunately we don't get to hear a whole lot about him. After all this is the acrostic of the virtuous woman not the virtuous man. I only wish there had been a similar male-focused passage. Not only would it enable me to write book two in the series but also clearly correct any mistaken assumptions. However, what we do know about the man in her life is that he is willing to let her be herself. She is not only involved within the house but, as we shall discover, a businesswoman as well. He is constantly praising her as verse 28 brings out, and rewarding her.

In fact, verse 23 points out that he is a well-respected leader in the land. He is not some TV-watching chauvinistic slob. My guess is, he would be neither macho or emasculated; a sort of Tom Hanks with Mel Gibson overtones. The truth is that, as we all get a little bit closer to the men and women we were designed to be, we will also be helping our spouses, children and friends become who they were designed to be.

letter seven

zayin

Proverbs 31:16

"She considereth a field and buyeth it: with the fruit of her hands she planteth a vineyard."

[KJV]

"She sets her mind on an estate and acquires it. She plants her vineyard from her profits."

[JPS]

zayin

This verse is brilliant. It stabs a massive hole in the 'submit woman… keep your world confined to just your husband, children and home' religious, chauvinistic hot-air balloon. Stab is indeed the operative word here as the 'zayin' was a picture of a sword and if you look at it long enough you will be able to see it. Consequently the 'zayin' stood for aggressiveness. This lady is feisty; she's got a bit of attitude and every now and then comes out of her corner fighting.

First of all, as one translation states, "she sets her mind on an estate" or as the NIV puts it, 'considers'. She is thinking, planning, dreaming and then once a strategy has emerged she acts. Self-doubt is dissipated as she gives herself internal permission to succeed.

This is the way life is meant to be. What we see and ponder on the inside should eventually flow into action on the outside. There is a planning stage and there is a doing stage… no room for long term hesitation and procrastination. I am sure her family are her cheerleaders here, but even if they are not, her inward strength moves her forward.

Zig Ziglar would put it this way, 'She is designed for accomplishment, engineered for success and endowed with the seeds of greatness.' Anything less than this is simply not acceptable.

The key word is the word 'buyeth' or 'acquire', which in some versions of the Bible is translated 'seized'. It has a sense of energy to it, a going out and grabbing something. Forget <u>Little Women</u>, this is <u>Xena the Warrior Princess</u>. I can sense all the men out there getting either worried or excited, and so you should be. For when she sets her mind to do something she is going to do it; in this particular case, purchasing land and starting a small business.

Previously we discovered such characteristics as dependability and security. Here we see the other side of the coin, a risk taker, an entrepreneur, someone who is willing to try new things and accept new challenges. I once heard of a couple of ladies who were inspired by this particular verse to start their own small business. They talked to their husbands first of all to get their input and advice, but discovered their husbands were not equally as enlightened and thought their idea would never work. Yet this did not dissuade the ladies in question. They sat down one day, wrote out the purpose and the strategy, and called their new business, 'Virtuous Cleaners'. Their idea was to organise a domestic cleaning company that would pride itself on excellence. Within a year both their husbands were working for them!

Now some men, it seems, have a problem if their spouse begins to earn more money than they do. I think such a reaction is very strange. I, in fact, encourage my wife to earn more money than I as I have a gift for spending and require as much raw material as possible!

So, go for it girl. Start the new business, go to the night school, apply for the new position, learn the instrument, write the book. Whatever it is, at least give it a whirl. Take the sword out of the scabbard and begin to cut away the creepers of self-doubt, fear and disappointment. Go Xena!

letter eight

cheth

Proverbs 31:17

"*She girdeth her loins with strength, and strengtheneth her arms.*"

[KJV]

"*How briskly she girds herself to the task, how tireless are her arms.*"

[KNOX]

cheth

The Hebrew letter 'cheth' is very similar to the 'he' [verse 14], yet this time without the window. 'Cheth' in fact was a picture of an enclosure, a fence or a hedge. This verse seems to be reiterating the strength that is part of the character of the virtuous woman. It is an all-encompassing characteristic and we find her strength manifested in a wide range of ways throughout this passage.

The Hebrew letter here may be able to help us in understanding one of the reasons she is able to maintain such internal strength. She has built for herself, if you like, an enclosure, a fence or a wall. She will not allow others to smash in and walk through her life in such a way as to devalue who she is. This is not a wall to keep people out but simply a boundary. A boundary line that demarcates between what is and what is not acceptable. Emotional openness – yes; manipulation – no. Physical love – indeed; physical abuse – never. Being vulnerable not violated. Able to be talked to not trampled down.

Without this sense of boundary many women and for that matter, men, allow other people to define them and limit them. Often, in an attempt to meet an expectation of others, we stop being ourselves and start playing a role. To maintain such a persona over the long term will ultimately cause much damage both within and without.

I recently watched again, a great documentary called <u>Blue Eyed</u>. The American teacher, Jane Elliot, who was featured and has now become known around the world, was trying to teach her class of seven-year-olds against racial prejudice. She did this by separating the class between blue eyes and those without, and having them play out roles of superiority and inferiority on alternate days. She was amazed to see how much the ugliness of prejudice impacted what had been a happy community of seven-year-olds.

As a result of the success not only of the teaching method but of the documentary, she conducts training seminars around the world for many corporations. In a discussion during one such gathering a very pleasant mid-western girl in her late twenties, with blonde hair and sparkly eyes, giggled as she talked about her feelings. She was very sweet as she pretended to be both comical and unperturbed by the experience she had just been through. Jane Elliot stood right in front of her, very seriously and impassively, until she had finished. Miss Elliot then pointed a finger in the young lady's face and said with great strength and passion, "Can I tell you something, lady? Can I tell you something that will make a difference to your life over the next thirty years… get over cute! You are cute now and everyone thinks it is funny but when you are forty-two you will just be another broad and there will be a whole host of younger, sweeter things than you around that will take your job and win the superficial admiration of those around them. Get over cute. Get trained. Get competent and grow up!"

The moral of the story is that men have often 'infanticised' women, and women have often allowed themselves to act and speak this way because it has been the predominant model. Yet this virtuous woman would resist such pressure. She is strong and self defined and would encourage all to build their enclosure by standing tall, being mature, professional and self-aware.

letter nine

teth

Proverbs 31:18

"*She perceiveth that her merchandise is good:
her candle goeth not out by night.* "

[KJV]

"*She knows the value of everything she makes
and works late into the night.* "

[GNB]

teth

The 'teth' is one of the more difficult letters to decipher, as there is no consensus as to what it was a picture of. Some authorities believe it was a picture of a snake or something that twists. If so, how does this apply to the virtuous woman and to the particular verse in question?… I haven't got the foggiest idea!

The snake, of course, has got quite a bit of theological baggage. Indeed one has to look far and wide, within not just Christian literature but most literature, to find positive references to this slithering reptile. Even Indiana Jones didn't like it.

It reminds me of the story of a rabbit who happened to meet a Diamondback Rattlesnake in the middle of the desert one day:

'Excuse me', said the rabbit, 'because I live in a desert, I've never seen water. I've got no idea what kind of animal I am because I've never seen myself. Would you be able to describe me and then I would be able to work out what I am?'

The snake replied, 'Certainly, but I as well don't know what kind of animal I am. After I describe you, will you describe me?'

They both agreed and the snake began. 'Well, you're white and fluffy. You've got big pink ears, a little bobbed tail and you hop.'

'I must be a rabbit,' said the rabbit.

'What about me?' said the snake.

'Well,' said the rabbit, 'you are low to the ground, you have squinty eyes, you speak with a forked tongue and you're covered with diamonds.'

'Oh no,' said the snake. 'I must be a televangelist!'

What has this to do with the virtuous woman? Not a lot but it was a joke worth telling.

One of the few positive comments on the snake comes from the Gospel of Matthew, chapter 10, verse 16, when Jesus encourages us to be as shrewd, or as cunning as snakes, yet as harmless as doves. Certainly the virtuous woman exemplifies this kind of wisdom.

Even though things are going well, 'she sees that her trading is profitable'. She does not rest on her laurels. She recognises that momentum is built when one adds energy to an already moving object. The time to double one's efforts is not when things are going badly but when things are going well. So in her case, even though her business is being successful, 'her lamp does not go out at night.' She is giving careful attention to maintaining the discipline of thinking and preparation because she realises we are never so vulnerable as when we are flushed with success.

One of my Bible School teachers compared this verse to Proverbs 20, verse 27, which in some translations seems to suggest that the human heart is God's lamp, that He leads and directs us from our inner world. Thus, in this particular verse, her lamp not going out at night was seen to mean her spiritual walk with God remained strong and consistent. Certainly it is true that when the going gets tough, people are often forced into a closer walk with God. There is nothing like a few trials and a bit of desperation to drive you to prayer. As the witticism goes, "Well, we had better pray…" "Why? Has it got that bad?"

Yet when our world is rosy, when businesses work, marriages prosper and churches grow, it is easy to forget about our reliance on God and begin to think that maybe we are responsible. Charles Spurgeon once stated that the person who doesn't pray must be a conceited individual to think he could do God's work on his own. Lack of prayer, the slow cooling of the heart to God, the diminishing of the spiritual lamp are all signs of self-satisfaction and personal smugness. Let us be smart enough to walk with God, not only through the valley of the shadow of death, but also in the green pastures and beside the quiet waters. After all, anybody can begin to pray when the chips are down; it takes someone of virtue to pray as a result of the relationship within rather than the circumstances without.

letter ten

yod

Proverbs 31:19

"She layeth her hands to the spindle, and her hands hold the distaff."

[KJV]

"Her hands are busy spinning thread, her fingers twisting fibre."

[NLT]

yod

The 'yod' is a picture of a clenched fist or, if you prefer, a closed hand. Certainly the latter sounds a lot more Christian! In particular it is the hand closed or the fist clenched in order to work. Notice how the verse itself parallels this perfectly.

The 'yod' is in fact Hebrew's smallest letter and the only letter suspended in mid-air. Jesus referred to it when he declared, 'that every jot and tittle of God's Word would come to pass[vi].'

Here in verse 19 the virtuous woman is still working on the clothes that she began in verse 13. For any of my readers who lack the necessary 5th Century BC knitting vocabulary, the distaff was the staff or rod on which the ball of yarn or flax was wound. And the spindle was part of the spinning wheel equipment used to spin the yarn. Both hands are involved in the detailed work of spinning wool or flax.

The virtuous lady, then, understands the importance of hard work and never shrinks back from it. Yet, as we discovered from the previous verse, she draws her strength from her relationship with God.

An interesting point to take note of is that the 'tittle' here, referring to the letter 'yod', was also used as the number ten. The Hebrews don't use numbers as we do but each letter corresponds to a various number, 'Aleph' being 1, 'Beth' being the 2 etc, and 11 being made up of a 'yod' 10 plus an 'Aleph' 1. The only time this numbering system breaks down is with the numbers 15 and 16 when 'yod-he' or 'yod-vah' would spell half of the holy name of God 'yahweh'. So to avoid this, the numbers 15 and 16 in Hebrew are the combinations of 6 and 9, and 7 and 9 respectively.

In light of the picture of 'yod' being that of the working hand, and also signifying the number 10, I find it fascinating to realise that when God created the world and did His work it was accomplished through ten divine utterances. Indeed there were ten things created on the first day

An equally engrossing parallel to this is that of the scriptural principle of tithing [i.e. giving one tenth back to God]. The Biblical promise was that if the individual undertook this, then God would infuse His strength into ours, His work into our work, thus prospering us beyond our own ability. If you like, it is the financial actualisation of Psalm 27 verse 1, "The Lord is the strength of my life. Of whom shall I be afraid?" Or as the New Testament puts it, "Be strong in the Lord and in the power of His might." With the demands of time and the pressures that face today's woman, it would be foolish to try to go it alone. Indeed the best way to not only survive but move ahead is to daily draw on God's divine strength. We are all, in fact, partners together with Him.

This wise woman is smart enough not to either work herself into a frazzle relying purely on her own strength, or be deceived into the opposite error; that of letting go of the spindle and the distaff, relaxing her energy and letting God do it all. I have discovered that we discover His strength when, with an attitude of faith, we come to the end of our own. It is a sensation the lazy and, for that matter, the workaholic will never enjoy.

letter eleven

kaph

Proverbs 31:20

"She stretcheth out her hands to the poor, yea, she reacheth forth her hands to the needy."

[KJV]

"Kindly is her welcome to the poor, her purse ever open to those in need."

[KNOX]

kaph

Another letter and another picture of a hand. This time, however, the 'kaph' is the open hand or the hollow of the hand. As both hands are involved in working, so both hands are involved in giving. Indeed one of the purposes of working is that there might be resources to give. The giving, however, implies more than just finances. Hands are not purely for the passing over of money but also for the embracing of the downhearted, the encouraging of the fallen and the praying for the sick.

The fact that these two verses come side by side gives me the impression that much of the motivation for her work [which includes, as you remember, not purely within the household, but also in business – both in real estate and viticulture] comes from this gift of giving. It would be correct to assume that the needs of her family are primary but beyond that there is much to do.

Philippians Chapter 2 verse 4 emphasises this as well. 'Each of you should look not only to your own interest, but also to the interest of others.' I think this is more than simply, 'I've been successful, let me now be generous.' Rather it is in the category,'I want to be generous. I want to make a difference. Therefore I have to be successful.'

One of the great truths of biblical Christianity is that the joy of giving, of living for others, of having goals bigger than oneself, is what life is really all about. Multiple homes, cars or boats, begs the question… why? Is this self-absorption, boredom, or loneliness? Am I trying to buy esteem, friends, respect? There is coming a new breed of business person whom many churches are recognising as Kingdom Builders. That is, people who have definite goals and aspirations to build successful business enterprises so that they can build the Kingdom. To be blessed in order to be a blessing.

Their spiritual DNA is reasonably specific. They see giving as their primary gift and faithfully obey Luke 6:38, "Give, and it will be given to you. A good measure, pressed down, shaken together and running over…". However, rather than viewing the "running over" as a gentle overflow they see it as a torrent. And in light of this see themselves as channels of God's resources rather than simply containers of it.

They understand that giving is not seasonal. Certainly there are times when resources are more plentiful, however, their giving comes from an inner calling rather than fortunate circumstances. Bad times don't stop their generosity. Good times simply increase the zeroes on the end of the figures. They have an in-built desire to continue to grow, to increase and to prosper. Not for selfish reasons but so they can be more effective in resourcing the local church.

Unlike many others the Kingdom Builder understands how the financial world works. That money and resources are acquired to release people into ministry, provide transportation, facilities and technology. The money is not the end, just a means – however, a vital means. Such ladies were involved in Jesus' ministry; Mary, Joanna and Susanna. "These women were helping to support Jesus and the disciples out of their own means." Luke 8:3

Finally, the demeanour of one who has this gift of giving is one of high gratefulness. Grateful people are generous people. The woman who lavished upon Jesus her expensive perfume in Luke 7:36-50 did so because she had been forgiven much. The self-pitying complainers will always be stingy for they are looking at what they haven't got. The grateful person gives freely, thrilled with the opportunity to do so.

I believe wise churches should encourage these kind of people, give them permission to prosper and then continually focus them on what it is all about – resourcing the Kingdom of God and meeting the needs of the desperate and the downtrodden. The virtuous woman of Proverbs would be quick to align herself with such a group.

letter twelve

lamedh

Proverbs 31:21

"She is not afraid of the snow for her household: for all her household are clothed with scarlet."

[KJV]

"She has no fear of winter for her household, for she has made warm clothes for all of them."

[LB]

lamedh

The 'lamedh' was a picture of an ox goad. No home should be without one! Today few of us have oxen and even fewer of us have 'goads'. Yet the word still remains in the sense of 'goading' – 'goading someone on to do something'.

The ox goad was an implement that had two purposes. First to prod the oxen on with a sharp point so they did not stop in the middle of ploughing. However, the end of the goad, which was shaped as a small sickle, served to clean the plough from time-to-time from large clods of earth or weed.

The only other reference I have found to an ox goad is in Acts Chapter 9 verses 4 & 5 when Jesus is speaking to Saul and declares, "Saul, Saul, why do you persecute me? It's hard to kick against the pricks [literally 'goads']." The virtuous woman then, has the ability to keep the family moving through tough times… as a result she is 'not afraid of the snow.' In fact, she is prepared ahead of time, having already clothed her family appropriately.

Snow makes for beautiful scenery but if you are not ready for it the winter blasts can be calamitous. Indeed, the snow could stand for the seasonal crises that come to every family. She is alert and ready before the first flakes descend to the ground. The quiet conversation with the daughter pre the adolescent relationship crash, the stern words to her husband as she perceives an over-confidence that could lead him into foolhardy decisions. Whatever it is, she has developed the ability to see it before it happens rather than when it is too late.

Much has been written on women's intuition. Certainly the virtuous woman excels in this area. When problems are imminent she is aware of them and prepares accordingly; 'Her whole house is clothed in crimson.'

A fascinating detour can be enjoyed by examining the word 'crimson'. It was a distinct colour that came from a crushed worm! Mainly used for expensive attire and predominantly the royal garments. The crimson dye extracted thus was highly prized. The worm in question was in Hebrew the 'tola'. The word only appears a handful of times in the Old Testament; probably the best known reference is Psalm 22:6. This Messianic Psalm has the suffering saviour crying out "I am a worm".

Literally, "I am a tola." The blood of Christ enables us all to wear kingly garb.

letter thirteen

mem

Proverbs 31:22

"She maketh herself coverings of tapestry: her clothing is silk and purple."

[KJV]

"She quilts her own bedspreads. She dresses like royalty in gowns of finest cloth."

[NLT]

mem

The 'mem' originally was simply a wavy line and was a picture of water. Over the years it has been modified into the letter we have today. Water has many connotations and meanings. Yet, the predominant meaning in Proverbs has to do with sexuality, as seen in Proverbs Chapter 5 verse 15, "Drink water from your own cistern, running water from your own well." This verse invokes the metaphor of a covered well to describe the virgin, and the next verses, 16 to 18; go on to say:

"Should your springs overflow in the streets, your streams of water in the public places? Let them be yours alone, never to be shared with strangers. May your fountain be blessed. May you rejoice in the wife of your youth."

These words extol the young man to not allow his streams [sexual energy] to be spread abroad.

The teaching of this verse corresponds well to the symbolism, 'Her clothing is linen and purple.' This probably refers to undergarments or, as we would say, fine lingerie. The coverings referred to are only mentioned one other time in Proverbs, in Chapter 7 verse 16; "I have covered my bed with coloured linens from Egypt." This is where the prostitute, in attempting to seduce a young man, describes her bed coverings of tapestry. The same word is used here in Proverbs Chapter 31.

Well, now that you are all hot and bothered, let us continue… this virtuous woman is certainly not a prude. Her sexuality is strong, healthy and unashamed. The trouble with living in a permissive culture is that not only is sexuality diminished and devalued, but that healthy, robust eroticism is tainted. Many Christians, in an endeavour to walk in sexual purity, find themselves unhealthily repressed when it comes to the whole purpose of sex – marital intimacy.

Growing up I learned through various Bible teachers that the Bible, Song of Solomon, was a metaphor of Christ and the Church. That every phrase of its poetic language had deep and spiritual nuances. Yet today I disagree with this interpretation. The more I have studied and thought about it, the more I am convinced that it is an erotic love poem celebrating the joy and wonder of sexuality. Other interpreters, by and large, seem to be trying to get away from the obvious. God created male and female, designed sex and deemed it all very good. What is more, He inspired a book that joys in it, which in turn is found worthy enough to be included in the canon of scripture… brilliant!

The virtuous woman then is sexually alive and vibrant. She dresses for her husband in the finest lingerie. She prepares herself and her bed. Sex is not an afterthought or a duty. It is a joy to be revelled in, a pleasure to be prepared for. In short, a gift from God.

Sex should be, indeed must be, passionate. The virtuous woman exemplifies this value. She is adventurous yet discreet; sensuous yet pure. She is for her man and he for her and together they make music in the night.

letter fourteen

nun

Proverbs 31:23

"Her husband is known in the gates, when he sitteth among the elders of the land."

[KJV]

"Her husband is a man of note in the public place, when he takes his seat among the responsible men of the land."

[BAS]

nun

The Hebrew letter 'nun' is a picture, believe it or not, of a fish. And the fish throughout ancient cultures stood for concentration - something I need to do after writing that last chapter!

Vestiges of this still remain. For example, have you played the card game that involves laying all the cards face down, scattered across the floor, and then choosing pairs, trying to remember where everything is, so as to turn over two of the same card? In Australia the game is called concentration. In England it is called fish. Not only that, but worldwide, the old saying, 'fish is good for the brain,' adds evidence to the Hebrew pictograph.

The verse itself seems to be saying that her husband is successful in what he is doing due to her. He is able to concentrate on the job at hand because he knows all is well at home. His success, in other words, is due to focus and that focus is only possible because he is married to a virtuous woman. This is in sharp distinction to the man referred to by Henry Youngman when he said, 'You know what it means to come home at night to a little bit of love, a little bit of affection? It means you've come back to the wrong house – that's what it means!'

This is not the case here. He obviously has the raw materials necessary for success… diligence, hard work and wisdom. However, due to the fact that he is partnered in life with such a lady his skills are enhanced, his confidence is encouraged and his ability to grow as a person and find fulfilment and meaning on life's journey are assured. He is better because of her and indeed she is better because of him. Rather than competing against each other or trying to control one another, they both work at releasing each other to be everything they should be. At the same time they maintain the strongest commitment to doing life together.

She is the foundation to her husband's success. The virtuous husband, of course, realises this and is quick to praise her and point this out. Indeed, modern statistics show that a happy marriage will lead to a longer, happier and more successful life. So, husbands, fathers, sons – concentrate, not just on who you are and what you have to do, but upon the women in your life! Admire them, honour them, invest in them and you will share in all their rewards!

letter fifteen

samech

Proverbs 31:24

"She maketh fine linen, and selleth it; and delivereth girdles unto the merchant."

[KJV]

"She designs gowns and sells them, brings the sweaters she knits to the dress shops."

[THE MESSAGE]

samech

The 'samech' was a picture of a fulcrum, a balance point or, if you like, the thing in the middle of the see-saw that makes it all work. Here, the industriousness of the virtuous woman (which we have seen in verses 13 and 19) now begins to pay off. We discover not only was she clothing the family, but making enough to sell besides. Due to the quality of the garments, selling is no problem. In a similar fashion (pardon the pun), Lydia in the New Testament was in the clothing business (Acts 16:14). The idea that the man of the house should be the sole provider certainly doesn't come from Proverbs. No, she brings balance and support to the house on several different levels with financial input being singled out here. If marriage is seen as a partnership, then responsibility should be shared in all areas: from looking after the home, providing resources, planning the finances and raising the children. Unfortunately, in many societies, tasks are divided up into 'his stuff' and 'her stuff'… no overlap allowed. Yet such an arrangement – although easier to set up – is fatally flawed. Not only is a job or responsibility attended to more successfully when two heads are involved, but in so doing, real partnership is forged. Besides that, the fun of cooking together in the kitchen will carry over to what is cooking in the bedroom as well! The wisdom of such a strategy is clearly seen when a spouse dies prematurely. In such tragic cases, the surviving partner at least has a fair idea of what is happening and needs to be done in every area of the household. There is a myriad of stories of left-behind husbands or wives that haven't got a clue regarding insurances, mortgage payments or maths homework. I'm not contending here that everything be divided neatly down the middle. Such a policy is rarely pragmatic and does not take into account each party's varied schedules, passions or talents. I am simply saying that both need to be involved in some way in each separate part of what makes a family and a marriage successful. In this way, we support one another and bring balance to one another.

One of the best selling marriage books in the last ten years was <u>His Needs, Her Needs</u> by Willard Harley.[vii] His study, years of counselling experience and most of all listening to thousands of couples, taught him some key truths. Primary among them was that we all have different needs. Obviously there are some exceptions, but in general women want, according to Harley, affection, conversation, honesty and openness, financial support and a strong commitment from her spouse to family. He, on the other hand, wants, in order of importance; sexual fulfilment, recreational companionship, an attractive spouse, domestic support and admiration… how superficial is that! What is most interesting about these two lists is that not one thing made it to both.

The point… we are different. Therefore it is easy to drift apart, so we have to cling together and work at meeting each other's varied needs. With only one person's perspective permitted, our vision will always be 50% impaired.

letter sixteen

ayin

Proverbs 31:25

"Strength and honour are her clothing; and she shall rejoice in time to come."

[KJV]

"Strength and dignity are her clothing and her position is strong and secure; she rejoices over the future [the latter day or time to come, knowing that she and her family are in readiness for it]!"

[AMP]

ayin

The 'ayin' was a picture of the eye, although some authorities link it also to a symbol representing a fountain of water. Indeed, both of these thoughts have application to this verse. The virtuous woman is a lady who sees differently. Her eyes look forward, not back. Her vision is for what will be, what could be; not on what was, and the sad regret of the passing years.

Vision, of course, is not an optical thing. "We see", as William Blake put it, "not with, but through the eye."[viii] In other words, vision is about how we think and interpret the visual information that enters our brain via the optic nerve. It has always been amazing to me how two people can observe the same phenomenon, and yet see different things. This is because vision is not purely objective but subjective as well. We see what we want to see; we see what we are looking for. Whether we, like her, look to the future with joy or foreboding has everything to do with us and little to actually do with our future. The truth is, of course, as we change the way we see things so the picture, the reality, begins to bend… like a slowly morphing image and so casts its ever-increasing light upon our lives. [ix]

The secondary picture of a fountain carries the meaning of inner strength. Water that bursts up to the surface comes from deep within and comes with energy and pressure. It is the same concept that Jesus spoke about when he said that eternal life would be a "spring of water welling up"[x] inside us. The strength of the virtuous woman, although seen on the outside, for she wears it as her garb, comes from the soul. Today's media culture and fashion magazine world suggest of course the exact opposite. Yet the need of the hour is for the heart-lift, not the face-lift. Beauty and vibrancy are internal qualities that exude from the virtuous woman in mesmerising and mysterious ways. Her dance, laughter and perspective start on the inside and flow without, bringing refreshment and sparkle to all around.

The Apostle Peter, in his letter, conveyed the same thought when he declared, "Your beauty should not come from outward adornment... instead, it should be that of your inner self…"[xi] External adornment is not seen as wrong, simply as secondary. The angry bitter heart cannot be covered up with multiple layers of foundation, whilst the strong and healthy soul will find that Estée Lauder may bring slight improvement in the same way that the extra ribbon enhances an already beautiful gift.

This, of course, explains how the virtuous lady can 'look to the future with cheer'. It was another Biblical writer who pointed out that the outward person is perishing in the aging process, but the inward person is growing, maturing and being renewed.*xii* Age is not to be frowned upon if it is adding to our life, yet, if we define ourselves as bodies alone, then the passing of each year is seen to devalue who we are. The virtuous woman discerns the difference. She is who she is within; therefore she looks to the future with joy, for tomorrow she will be stronger and wiser. She realises that we do not stop playing, dreaming, thinking and growing because we are old; we grow old because we stop playing, dreaming, thinking and growing.

letter seventeen

p e

Proverbs 31:26

"She openeth her mouth with wisdom; and in her tongue is the law of kindness."

[KJV]

"When she speaks she has something worthwhile to say, and she always says it kindly."

[THE MESSAGE]

pe

The 'pe' is a picture of the open mouth and, unlike many of the letters, can still be seen in its present form. This dovetails perfectly with what is being said in the verse, "She openeth her mouth with wisdom; and in her tongue is the law of kindness." She is not simply nattering away, filling her time with useless gossip or superficial small talk. She realises that one of her roles is to instruct, educate and input into the lives around… her spouse, her friends and, most of all, her children. Kindly wisdom is echoed much later in the New Testament with the phrase, 'speaking the truth in love' .[xiii] The right word can be delivered in the wrong way and, as a result, its wisdom squandered. In Proverbs 25:11, this idea is expanded upon, 'A word fitly spoken is like apples of gold in settings of silver.' This is an example of a picture parallelism. That is, one line of this proverb gives the teaching and the other is a picture of that teaching. The trick is to work out how the picture illustrates the teaching. In this particular case, the teaching has two elements, 'A word fitly spoken'. What is said… 'the word', and how it is said, the occasion, tone and attitude… in which it is given… 'fitly'. The picture here also contains two elements, 'apples of gold in settings of silver', or, as the Living Bible puts it, "golden apples in a silver basket." Golden apples are obviously more valuable than the silver basket. In the same way that the word spoken, the truth, is more important than where or how it is said. Yet both are required, the word and the fitly, the truth and the love, the picture and the frame, to effectively communicate the message and leave a lasting impression. The scolding correction will never influence to the same level as the gentle reproof. The truth-telling yet caustic person is simply not being wise, because wisdom understands that love, gentleness or empathy are what one needs to actually transplant wisdom from one person to the next. The life, the manner, gives credibility to the lesson. The virtuous lady then doesn't just know her stuff – she also consistently lives the kind of life and approaches the teaching moments in such a way as to create willingness in the heart of the hearer. Something which the contentious woman (often mentioned throughout Proverbs) fails to grasp.

letter eighteen

tsadat

Proverbs 31:27

"She looketh well to the ways of her household, and eateth not the bread of idleness."

[KJV]

"She keeps an eye on everyone in her household, and keeps them all busy and productive."

[THE MESSAGE]

tsadat

The picture here, like the previous verse, is still recognisable from the Hebrew letter. Unfortunately for many people, that doesn't help, as what it's a picture of is something that is reasonably rare. In fact, it's one of those old fashioned scythes - a reaping hook or a sickle, as it is called in some parts of the world. One held on to the two handles at the top, and the bottom part of the letter was the blade. Growing up on a farm in Kent, England, I well remember getting blisters on one of these as I attempted to hack my way through a field of bracken and stinging nettles. In biblical times, the scythe was the primary harvesting implement, the sound of its gentle swish would fill the land when the crops were ready. We can actually apply this particular image to the rest of the acrostic, for from Verse 27 on, everything that is expanded upon has to do with the virtuous lady's harvest in life. Her discernment, the reaction of her husband and children, her wisdom and, finally, the legacy she leaves, the mark she makes upon her world.

The key word here is 'watches', and carried the idea of practical and spiritual alertness. The Living Bible has it, "she watches carefully", whilst

Luther paraphrases this as, "she looks how it goes in her house". As one commentator explains, "her eyes are turned everywhere", and since this time, mothers everywhere have used this picture to their own advantage. I know my mother certainly did, 'I've eyes at the back of my head', she used to say. My young brain knew this to be anatomically incorrect, yet deep within, I felt its truth. Forget Big Brother… Big Mother is watching you! Yet, this watching is not the watching of an angry schoolmaster… it is preventional. She is on guard for potential problems. Spiritually, she is tuned in and can pick up, before anybody else in the family, when trouble or danger is in the air. This is why husbands do well to listen. Many a rash decision leading to some form of misfortune could have been averted if her wise intuition had been heeded. Indeed, she has the type of wisdom that we call discretion; that is the wisdom that keeps one out of future problems.

Laziness, as the second part of this Verse points out, destroys this kind of spiritual sensitivity. Life is very much like this… the more we put in, the more we get out. The diligent and the disciplined experience self worth and prosperity, peace and effectiveness. Those who shun sloth discover all sorts of benefits along their way. On the other hand, a lazy heart dulls the mind and desensitises the spirit. The voice of God comes to those who are busy… whether it is Elisha, ploughing in a field, or Joseph working hard in a prison; those who put their shoulders to the wheel are rewarded in surprising and ever increasing ways.

letter nineteen

qoph

Proverbs 31:28

"Her children arise up, and call her blessed;
her husband also, and he praiseth her."

[KJV]

"Her sons congratulate her, and thus her
husband praises her."

[MOF]

ק

qoph

I think 'qoph' would have to be my favourite Hebrew letter... not only does its aesthetics please... flowing lines, sensuous curves, but also its sound... 'qoph' [pronounced koof]. I have always imagined it to be the sound of impact if one fell off a 20-storey building into a giant marshmallow. It is a picture of the head or, more specifically, the back of the head. Here we find that the praise the virtuous woman receives is behind her back. The idea here is not that the husband and children are talking to her, but talking about her to third parties. "The children arise" [or we could read 'grow up'] "and call her blessed." The problem with being a child is you never know how your parents rate. One only realises one has had a healthy or dysfunctional upbringing when one is old enough to analyse, compare and discern. Great mums are only really appreciated when their kids realise they are great – something which can take, in many cases, three decades or more. Yet the promise here is that they will arise and call her blessed. With maturity will come insight. Praise may be delayed, but it is on the way.

One of the keys to a successful marriage is to put your spouse on a pedestal. Certainly, this is what her husband is doing. One can imagine him bragging to his friends and colleagues about how wonderful she is and, I'm sure, his remarks are met with feigned incredulity and jovial exclamation… "What did she ever see in you?" "You obviously married above yourself." Doubtless, this marriage had been arranged which, contrary to popular culture, led more often than not to successful endings. As one Indian scholar remarked, "In the West you marry the one you love; in the East we love the one we marry." Love is that which is decided upon, learnt about, grown in and then felt; beginning with simply feeling is more often than not a recipe for short-term infatuation rather than lifelong partnership. The chorus of praise and honour increases as the years go by and the circle of her influence continues to widen as her husband and her children find their way in the world. Recognition and respect ripple out and thus her harvest increases.

letter twenty

resh

Proverbs 31:29

"*Many daughters have done virtuously, but thou excellest them all.*"

[KJV]

"*Many women have done wonderful things, but you've outclassed them all!*"

[THE MESSAGE]

resh

Qoph was an image of the back of the head. Resh is one of the front – the forehead. Praise is wonderful when it is shared abroad, yet honouring people to their faces is of paramount importance. The idea of Verse 29 is that the husband is speaking these words to his virtuous woman. In effect, he is saying that there may be many wonderful women in the world, yet he is privileged to be married to the best. While others are consumed with doubt… "Maybe I married the wrong person", "Someone more suited could have been just around the corner"; he boldly declares… "You are the one". The sense of security such proclamation brings to a relationship simply fertilises the ground for more and richer fruit.

I heard once of a certain South Seas Island custom of paying the dowry for one's wife in cows. An average bride was worth two to three cows, the exceptional up to six. Yet, the story was told of a certain suitor who paid eight cows for what was considered a reasonably plain girl. The whole village (except, of course, this particular girl's father) thought the prospective husband had taken leave of his senses. "Eight cows…

he definitely could have won her hand with three." Yet his esteem, love and public declaration of her worth had a powerful effect. For, after the marriage, she grew in confidence and grace until everyone began to realise she was indeed an eight-cow wife. How we are viewed is an important catalyst in becoming who we are meant to be, especially when such praise is to our face. Unfortunately, honestly expressing our respect, admiration or love for someone is something the majority shy away from. We give flowers to the dead, rarely to the living; yet the living need them. Indeed, our souls are nourished and fed through the genuine insight and input of others. This truth is of course gender-free. In fact men need this kind of therapy as much, if not more, than women… you see we have frail egos, despite our ramboic exteriors, we crave admiration and, when we receive it, we become little boys again, malleable and easily directed according to the whims and desires of our lady!

letter twenty one

shin

Proverbs 31:30

"Favour is deceitful, and beauty is vain:
but a woman that feareth the Lord,
she shall be praised."

[KJV]

"Charms may wane and beauty wither, keep
your praise for a wife with brains."

[MOF]

shin

This letter is another of the few that are still recognisable as pictographs. The image is one of a tooth… a molar to be exact – a chewing tooth as opposed to a cutting one. Consequently, its meaning is closely associated with our thinking… what we chew over in our minds. Thus, this Verse concentrates on what the virtuous woman concentrates on. Its content is the subject of her meditation. Since ancient times, it's been understood that what a person thinks about frames their whole life. In short, we are not what we think we are, but what we think… we are.

This fact, in itself, is highly significant. The mind operates like a neural road system. The way we think creates certain roads, ones that we travel frequently, multi-laned with no exits. A new thought ventures into an unknown wasteland where its path is one that is hacked out of virgin jungle. Thus, once we think a certain way we are hooked. 'I am not very clever so I will probably not do well in life.' Or, 'I am feeling depressed so let me get another drink.' These become habitual patterns of thought leading to habitual patterns of behaviour. As a result we will continue to follow the familiar cerebral road with increasing ease and rapidity. Our neural architecture then can help build our lives or aid in their destruction.

So, what is it then that is the subject of the virtuous woman's ponderings?

We have already discovered that she lives from the inside out; that her confidence, strength and spirituality are found first within, then seen without. This Verse, in two sentences, summarises the central philosophy of her life and gives insight into how she moves with such grace and attitude, not only through the daily ups and downs of existence, but also in dealing with the passing of the years. "Elegance is a lie and dazzling looks are fleeting, but a woman who fears the Lord will be praised." She has worked out that an externally driven life is empty. Cellulite-free, wrinkleless bodies last only for a short time, yet the inner world of beauty beams brighter and brighter. The meaning of life is deeper than the physical reality of an aging body. We are not our bodies… they are simply earth suits, necessary for existence, worthy of attention and decoration, but not our worship.

"She fears the Lord." Here we discover the inner core of her world. Her vibrant relationship with God fuels her human psyche in such a way that the deep yearning for meaning and fulfilment are met and her life is set free to celebrate and savour the gift of being. She is grateful for she knows who she is. She is steadfast for she knows whose she is. She is hope-filled for life for her extends beyond the curtain of mortality and is nourished by this faith in her unseen yet undeniable God. This is what she thinks upon, therefore this is how she lives and her life bears fruit to the truth and wonder of such thoughts.

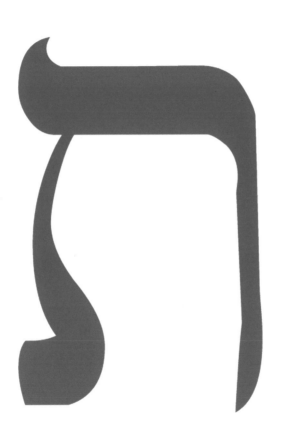

letter twenty two

tau

Proverbs 31:31

"Give her of the fruit of her hands; and let her own works praise her in the gates."

[KJV]

"Give her everything she deserves! Festoon her life with praises!"

[THE MESSAGE]

tau

So we reach the conclusion of Proverbs mini essay on the woman of virtue. The Hebrew alphabet culminates with letter 22 - the tau, which appropriately carries the meaning of a signature. The closing mark on the end of a treatise, statement or correspondence. In this case, the letter is the life and the signature is borne by her husband and children. She has marked them and, even after she is gone, her legacy continues to be seen, heard and felt.

In life, we all leave our mark. For some of us, it is quickly obscured by the passing of time, yet significant deeds from the lives of significant people continue to echo through the ages. I'm not just talking here of the celebrity, the well-known individual whose media, videos or songs remind us globally of their existence. Such a life may be more visible but the recollections all too shallow. The life that is significant is so because it has actually made a difference within its sphere of influence. Virtue is not measured by how many people know about it but by the depth and meaning of that knowledge. Mother Teresa is well known; there are countless others with the same devotion whose impact is only felt in a remote village or extended family. In the words of Shakespeare, a life which causes memory to 'take its seat'.

Integrity has its rewards. Sowing leads to reaping, and the life of the virtuous woman produces a chorus of approval as this Verse declares… 'let her own works praise her in the gates'. One of my dreams is to be one day sitting around a super large family table filled with our children, their spouses, and our grandchildren, with various aunts and uncles, friends and colleagues thrown in for good measure. To hear the children playing, smell the roast sizzling, and know this group of people are secure, prospering and wise because I was a good husband and father for forty years, and Heather, my wife, was this virtuous woman, who turned our house into a home, nourished us with her love and creativity, and guided us with her spiritual vigilance… and now we sit… growing sleepy in the afternoon sun, fulfilled, well content and happy. And I trust that when we are well gone, our grandchildren and great-grandchildren will continue the tradition lifting their glasses to the old dearly departed couple who built a good foundation and are now having an even better time.

"I struggled through the alphabet as if it had been a bramble bush, getting considerably worried and scratched by every letter."

Charles Dickens

GREAT EXPECTATIONS, 1861, CH. 7.

appendices

APPENDIX 1

The Picture of a Sound

Our alphabet is the evolution of a picture of a thing moving eventually to become the picture of a sound. Most of us are familiar with one set of these pictures that is used extensively today – the Roman alphabet. This alphabet is, in turn, used in different languages: English, Spanish, French, Italian, German etc. However, this set of pictures is only one set amongst many. The Chinese have a totally different group of symbols for sounds, as do the Japanese, Arabic and Jewish people.

All these letters were originally pictographs; that is, they were simply the pictures of things.

For example = house.

Slowly, due in part to the need for speed and also because most concepts or ideas do not lend themselves to the picture model, the ideograph was born as in:

= God.

The Sumerian originally was a pictograph for a star, but soon became a symbol for God (well, you try coming up with a picture for the Almighty!) The final stage for this evolution was the hieroglyph, when a picture was utilised for a sound as in 'Z' for the zed sound.

The first proper alphabet along these lines was probably Phoenician, on whose heels Hebrew quickly followed. The Hebrew alphabet – due to its early development – still has glimpses of the original pictures.

For example, the Hebrew letter [Beth] was taken from the Hebrew word for house, 'beit' and originally looked more like a house.

And the original picture of water morphed into the Hebrew letter, 'mem' for similar reasons.

APPENDIX 2

The Legend of Creation Letters

"Creation begins with a 'B', not 'agins' with an 'A'."
A B Kuhn

One of the more interesting legends concerning creation is how God chose which letter to begin the whole process

It was first recorded in the <u>Book of Splendour</u> [Sefer Ha-Zohar] written by Moses de Leon before the thirteenth century.

Ben Shalom in the <u>Alphabet of Creation</u> and later Richard Firmage in <u>Alphabet Abecedarium</u> retell the story:

> *'The twenty-two letters of the alphabet descended from the crown of God whereon they were engraved with a pen of flaming fire. They gathered around about God and one after another spoke and entreated, each one, that the world be created through him.' As God considered their various petitions, their*

merits and faults were linked with the meaning of words they begin. For example, 'Heth, although it is the first letter of Hanun, the Gracious One, is also first in the word for sin – Hattat. So the letter Heth was rejected... And Gimel, although it reminds one of Gadol, great, would not do, because it also stands at the head of Gemul – retribution.' Finally, the letter B [beth] applied for the honour. 'Beth stepped before the Holy one, blessed be He, and pleaded, 'O Lord of the World! May it be Thy will to create the world through me, seeing that all the dwellers in the world daily give praise unto Thee through me. For it is said, 'Baruch – blessed – be the Lord forever: Amen and Amen!' The Holy One, blessed be He, immediately granted the petition of Beth, saying, 'Blessed be he that cometh in the name of the Lord!' And He created the world through Beth; as it is said, 'Bereshith – in the beginning – God created the Heaven and the Earth.' [xiv]

Alphabetical Recitals

(these are sentences which, when read, sound like the alphabet but are in fact a sentence)

"Eh! Be Seedy, ye effigy ot shy Jake. "A lemon, opaque. "You are a stew ~ feed a bull you ex! "Why said."

Alan Symonds

"Abby seized Dee's effigy, hijacked Elle's minnow, piqued curest tease. "You're double~used", ex~wised zee."

Louis Phillips

"Hay, be seedy! He effigy, hate~shy. Jakey yellow man, o peek! You are rusty, you've edible you ex~wise he!"

Harry Matthews

"Rendered alphabetically,
a word remains strictly itself.
Rendered by means of pictograms,
ideograms and phonograms,
a word becomes something else
as well as itself."

Adonis and the Alphabet,
The Collected Works of Aldous Huxley

CHATEAU AND WINDUS, LONDON, 1979. P 191.

Endnotes

i   Other acrostics include: Lamentations Chapters 1-4, Nahum Chapter 1, Psalms 9, 10, 25, 34, 37, 111, 112, 119 and 145... Probably the best known one, Psalm 119, gives eight verses to each letter. Thus the first eight all begin with aleph, the next 8 with beth and so on and so forth. With this kind of design, this Psalm was always destined to be the longest one in the book. Many Bibles still include the letters before each set of eight verses.

ii   See Appendix 1 for a brief history of the Hebrew alphabet and the origin of pictographs.

iii "Husbands in the same way be considerate as you live with your wives, and treat them with respect as the weaker partner...". 1 Peter 3:7

iv   Blake, William, The Everlasting Gospel, Complete Writings of William Blake, lines 103-106, edited Geoffrey Keynes, Oxford University Press, London, 1966, pg. 753.

v   Baker, Phil, Attitudes of Amazing Achievers, Webb & Partners, Perth, 2000.

vi   *Matthew 5:18, King James Version.*

vii   *Harley, Willard F Jnr., <u>His Needs Her Needs</u>, Fleming H Revell Division of Baker Books, Grand Rapids, Michigan, 2001.*

viii   *Blake, William, The Everlasting Gospel, <u>Complete Writing of William Blake</u>, Lines 103-106, edited Geoffrey Keynes, Oxford University Press, London, 1966, pg. 753.*

ix   *For more information on the phenomenon of vision see the author's book, <u>Attitudes of Amazing Achievers</u>, Webb & Partners, Perth, 2000.*

x   *John 4:13 & 14.*

xi   *I Peter 3:4 & 5.*

xii   *II Corinthians 4:16.*

xiii   *Ephesians 4:15.*

xiv   *As told by Richard Firmage, <u>Alphabet Abecedarium</u>, Bloomsbury Publishing, London, 2000, pgs. 57 & 58.*

"The alphabet is
the tool of thought."

Marshall McLuhan

Selected Bibliography

The Collected Works of Aldous Huxley, Chateau and Windus, London 1979.

Alphabeta - How our Alphabet Shaped the Western World, John Mann, Headline Book Publishing, London, 2000.

The Alphabet - A Key to the History of Mankind, David Diringer, Hutchinson & Co, London, 1968.

Mysteries of the Alphabet, Marc-Alain Ovaknin, Abbeville Press Publishers, New York, 1999.

ABC Et Cetera - The Life and Times of the Roman Alphabet, Alexander and Nicholas Humez, David R Godine Publisher, Boston, 1985.

Making the Alphabet Dance, Ross Eckler, St Martins Press, New York, 1996.

Alphabet Abecedarium, Richard Firmage, Bloomsbury Publishing, London, 2000.

"Human society, the whole
of mankind, is in the alphabet."

Victor Hugo.

Translations

Amp:	Amplified Bible, Zondervan Publishing House, Grand Rapids, MI, 1965.
Bas:	The Bible in Basic English, Cambridge University Press & E.P. Dutton & Co.
Darby:	Darby Translation.
GNB:	Good News Bible, American Bible Society, New York, 1976.
JPS:	The Holy Scriptures according to the Masoretic Text: A New Translation, The Jewish Publication Society of America, 1955.
KJV:	King James Version.
Knox:	The Holy Bible: A Translation from the Latin Vulgate in the Light of the Hebrew and Greek Originals [Monsignor Ronald Knox], Sheed & Ward Inc. & Burns and Oats Ltd, New York, 1954.
LB:	Living Bible, Tyndale House Publishers, Wheaton, IL, 1971.
The Message:	The Message Translation, Navpress, Colorado Springs, CO, 1993.
Mof:	A New Translation of the Bible [James Moffatt], Harper and Row Publishers Inc. & Hodder & Stoughton Ltd, 1954.
NASB:	New American Standard Bible, International Bible Society, 1977.
NEB:	The New English Bible, Oxford University Press, 1961.
NLT:	New Living Translation, Tyndale House Publishers, 1996.
NIV:	New International Version, Zondervan Bible Publishers, Grand Rapids, MI, 1984.
YLT:	Youngs Literal Translation.

letters

to a lady

The Author

Phil Baker is the bestselling author of several books including Secrets Of Super Achievers and Wisdom – The Forgotten Factor Of Success.

He is also a renowned international speaker, speaking to business people, conferences and churches with audiences ranging from 50 to 10,000 people.

Phil lives in Perth, Australia, where he is the Senior Minister of Riverview Church, one of Australia's largest churches.

PHIL BAKER'S ON-LINE DIARY

Visit Phil Baker's on-line diary where he regularly posts his thoughts and observations on a range of topics from politics, history, philosophy, theology, poetry, running and more stuff!

You can visit his BLOG at www.philbaker.net

Additional Resources

YOUR INNER WORLD
Monthly CD Resource Programme with Phil Baker

BUILDING LEADERS AUDIO CD'S

OTHER BOOKS
Secrets of Super Achievers
Attitudes of Amazing Achievers
Wisdom of Wealthy Achievers
Wisdom – The Forgotten Factor of Success
The Journey
Weird Christians I Have Met

resources@riverviewchurch.com.au

www.riverviewchurch.com.au

"'Of course, you know your ABC?'
said the Red Queen.
'To be sure, I do,' said Alice.
'So do I,' the White Queen whispered.
'We'll often say it over together dear.
And I'll tell you a secret
~ I can read words of one letter!
Isn't that grand?
However, don't be discouraged.
You'll come to it in time.'"

Through The Looking Glass
Lewis Carroll

AVENIL BOOKS, P. 192.